Edmund White

Terre Haute

LEARNING CENTRE

Methuen Drama

Published by Methuen Drama, 2007

1 3 5 7 9 10 8 6 4 2

Methuen Drama
A & C Black Publishers Limited
38 Soho Square
London W1D 3HB
www.acblack.com

ISBN: 978 0 713 68794 1

A CIP catalogue record for this book
is available from the British Library

Typeset by Country Setting, Kingsdown, Kent
Printed in the UK by CPI Bookmarque, Croydon, CR0 4TD

Caution

nabokov presents

Terre Haute

by Edmund White

James	**Peter Eyre**
Harrison	**Arthur Darvill**
Directed by	**George Perrin**
Designed by	**Hannah Clark**
Lighting designed by	**Matthew Eagland**
Music composed by	**Heather Fenoughty**
Assistant Director	**Tara Wilkinson**
Producer	**James Grieve**
Edinburgh:	
Production Manager	**Ric Mountjoy**
Stage Manager	**Sarah Lyndon**
Production Assistant	**MaryClare O'Neill**
London and Tour:	
Production Manager	**Nick Fieldsend**
Company Stage Manager	**Christabel Anderson**
Tour Management	scamp
Press	**Cliona Roberts**
Photography	**Marc Brenner**

Terre Haute was first performed at The Assembly Rooms, Edinburgh,
on 5 August 2006

nabokov would like to thank: Sebastian Warrack and Arts Council England, East; Cat Moore, Anthony Roberts, Steve Forster and Escalator East To Edinburgh; Jenny, Louise and Dawn at SCAMP Theatre; Louise Chantal, Becky Singh and The Assembly Rooms; Angela Ayers at The Bowen West Theatre; LAMDA; Jo Luke; Nia Janis; Nic Fryer; Sam Grafton; Old Vic New Voices; English Touring Theatre; Tom Burke; Amy Ball; Imogen Kinchin; Roxana Silbert; Buddy Thomas.

ESCALATOR SUPPORTING ARTISTS IN THE EAST OF ENGLAND EAST TO EDINBURGH

nabokov

"Proving that political drama does have a place in the 21st Century"
The List

nabokov is a new writing theatre company dedicated to commissioning, developing and producing backlash theatre - new work that offers an antagonistic response to contemporary agendas, trends and events.

Since 2001, we have produced critically acclaimed productions in London, Edinburgh and on tour, including KITCHEN, BEDTIME FOR BASTARDS, CAMARILLA and NIKOLINA. Our World Premiere production of TERRE HAUTE debuted at The Assembly Rooms, Edinburgh, in August 2006.

We aim to develop new work through events, workshops, readings and literary programmes. Our monthly development forum, SHORTS, ran for five years in Sheffield, Manchester, Liverpool and London, offering cross-disciplinary artists the chance to test out new work in front of an audience. Our PRESENT : TENSE events challenge playwrights to write plays in response to the most important story on the news agenda in just one week.

Our latest commission, ARTIFACTS by Mike Bartlett, has recently been awarded the inaugural Old Vic New Voices Award for new writing and a Stage One / Society of London Theatres New Producer's Bursary.

nabokov is supported by Arts Council England, East, through its Escalator programme.

For **nabokov**:

Artistic Directors	**James Grieve and George Perrin**
Executive Director	**Ric Mountjoy**
Administrator	**Nic Wass**
Playwright-in-Residence	**David Dipper**
Associate Playwright	**DC Moore**

contact@nabokov-online.com // www.nabokov-online.com

TERRE HAUTE 2007

National Tour

10 - 11 April
Mercury Theatre, Colchester
(01206) 577006

13 April
Old Town Hall, Hemel Hempstead
(01442) 228091

14 April
Trestle Arts Base, St Albans
(01727) 850950

17 April
Darlington Arts Centre
(01325) 486555

18 April
The Junction, Cambridge
 (01223) 511511

19 April
the hat Factory, Luton
(01582) 878100

20-21 April
Bath Theatre Royal
(01225) 448844

24-28 April
Drum Theatre Plymouth
(01752) 267222

1 May
Norwich Playhouse
(01603) 598598

3-5 May
The Studio, Royal Exchange, Manchester
(0161) 8339833

West End

7 May - 2 June
Trafalgar Studios, London
(0870) 0606632

EDMUND WHITE

Edmund White is the author of twenty books including novels, short stories, essays, travel books and biographies. His magisterial biography of Jean Genet won the National Book Critics' Circle Award and his short biography of Marcel Proust was a best seller. His trilogy of autobiographical novels - *A Boy's Own Story*, *The Beautiful Room is Empty* and *The Farewell Symphony* - have become classics of contemporary gay literature. White has been called America's Marcel Proust and *Le Monde* compared him to Henry James. He is a member of the American Academy of Arts and Letters and an officer in the French Order of Arts and Letters. He lived in Paris for 16 years in the 1980s and 90s and his books - *Our Paris* and *The Flaneur: A Stroll Through the Paradoxes of Paris* - have won him a wide popular audience. He teaches creative writing at Princeton and lives in New York. His memoir, *My Lives*, was published last year to much acclaim. *Terre Haute* is his third play, developed at the Sundance Festival in Utah. In September 2007, Bloomsbury is publishing a new novel, *Hotel de Dream*.

THE COMPANY

CHRISTABEL ANDERSON (Company Stage Manager)

Christabel trained at The University of Edinburgh and LAMDA. Recent theatre credits include: *The Hound of the Baskervilles* (for Peepolykus, the West Yorkshire Playhouse and Neal Street Productions) and the national and international tour of *After the End* (a Bush / Paines Plough co-production). Other theatre credits include work with the Traverse Theatre, Clean Break and the Royal Court as well as a spell as Resident Stage Manager for the Bush Theatre in London. She has also worked on a number of occasions on *The Woman in Black* in the West End and was DSM for Christopher Biggins' pantomime company for five years. Opera credits include Grange Park, Garsington and Wexford Opera Festivals. Christabel has also Stage Managed events at Apothecaries' Hall, King's College and Shakespeare's Globe and she was involved in *Oklahoma!* at the Edinburgh Playhouse which set the Guinness World Record for the fastest ever theatrical production.

HANNAH CLARK (Designer)

Hannah trained in Theatre Design at Nottingham Trent University and, in 2005, completed an MA in Scenography with distinction at Central School of Speech and Drama for which she won an A.H.R.C. Award. She was a winner of the 2005 Linbury Biennial Prize for stage design. Theatre designs include: *Who's Afraid Of Virginia Woolf* (Royal Exchange, Manchester); *Big Love* (Gate Theatre, Notting Hill); *The Taming Of The Shrew* (Bristol Old Vic); *Jammy Dodgers* (Requardt & Company, The Place, London); *Death Of A Salesman*, *What The Butler Saw*, *Blue/Orange*, *A View From The Bridge*, *I Just Stopped By To See The Man*, *Two* and *Frankie And Johnny In The Clair De Lune* (Octagon Bolton). Future work includes: *We That Are Left* by Gary Owen at Watford Palace Theatre.

ARTHUR DARVILL (Harrison)

Arthur trained at RADA. Since graduating in 2006, he has worked on *Terre Haute* at the Assembly Rooms in Edinburgh, *The Verdict* for RDF Television and *Stacy* by Jack Thorne at the Arcola Theatre. Arthur is a founding member of Fuego's Men Theatre Company. He also performed in Ted Hughes' *Tales from Ovid* for Traumwand Theatre Company in Austria.

MATTHEW EAGLAND (Lighting Designer)
Theatre includes: *The Tempest* (Theatre Royal Bath); *Charley's Aunt* (Theatre Royal Bath); *Carrie's War* (Lilian Baylis Theatre); *Copenhagen* (Palace Theatre, Watford); *An Hour and a Half Late* (Theatre Royal, Bath); *It's a Fine Life* (Queen's Theatre, Hornchurch); *Terre Haute* (Assembly Rooms, Edinburgh); *The Scarlet Pimpernel* (London Children's Ballet); *A Room at the Top* (QTH); *Joking Apart* (Northcott Theatre, Exeter); *Macbeth* (QTH); *One Last Card Trick* (Watford Palace Theatre); *Private Lives* (Theatre Royal Bath Productions); *Cinderella* (QTH); *Alfie* (WPT); *Grind* (The Generating Company); *Darwin in Malibu* (Birmingham Rep); *Moon on a Rainbow Shawl* (Nottingham Playhouse); *One Under, John Bulls Other Island, Crossing Jerusalem, Ten Rounds, The Promise, A Night in November, The Wexford Trilogy* (The Tricycle); *Little Women* (Duchess Theatre); *Murderous Instincts* (Savoy Theatre); *Anne of Green Gables* (LBT); *Dancing at Lughnasa* (NT, Exeter); *Femme Fatale* (Warehouse Theatre); *My Boy Jack* (National Tour); *Much Ado About Nothing* (Bremer Shakespeare Company); *Christmas* (The Bush Theatre); *The Lieutenant of Inishmore* (National Tour); *A Taste of Honey, The Ghost Train, Brief Encounter, Sleuth, The Good Intent, Educating Rita* and *A View from the Bridge* (QTH); *Hay Fever* (Oxford Stage Company); *The Winter's Tale* (AandBC); *The Arbitrary Adventures of an Accidental Terrorist, Kes* (NYT); *Tape* (NVT, Brighton); *The Changeling, The Winter's Tale* (Southwark Playhouse); *Hamlet, The Winter's Tale, Confusions, Ghetto, The Pool of Bethesda, Cinderella* and *A Tale of Two Cities* (GSMD); *The Age of Consent* (Pleasance, Edinburgh); *Moving On* (The Bridewell). Opera: *La Traviata, L'Elisir di Amore* (English Touring Opera, Education); *La Finta Semplice, Jacko's Hour, The Long Christmas Dinner* and *The Dinner Engagement* (GSMD), *L'Heure Espagnol* and *Gianni Schicchi* (RSAMD). Future projects include *Around the World in 80 Days* for QTH, and *The Secret Garden* for London Children's Ballet.

PETER EYRE (James)

Peter made his stage debut with the Old Vic Company and did repertory seasons in Harrogate, Glasgow, Birmingham and two years in Nottingham where he played Edgar in *King Lear* (also Old Vic) and the Prince in *The Idiot*. He played Konstantin in *The Seagull* (Chichester Festival and Greenwich Theatre), Oswald in *Ghosts* and Hamlet in *Hamlet* (Greenwich Theatre), Axel in *Comrades*, Tim in *The Desert Air*, Toulon in *Red Noses* (RSC) and Tesman in *Hedda Gabla* (RSC Aldwych, also Australia, USA and Canada), Tusenbach in *The Three Sisters* (Cambridge Theatre), Ferdinanda in *A Country Life* (Lyric Hammersmith), Ronnie in *The Potsdam Quartet* (Lyric Hammersmith), Antiochus in *Berenice*, Pyrrhus in *Andromache* (Old Vic), Brunelli in *The Madman of the Balconies* (Gate Theatre), Polonius in *Hamlet* (Almeida and Broadway), *Chere Maitre* (Almeida and Flea Theatre, New York), Ken in *Smoking With Lulu* (West Yorkshire Playhouse). In recent years he has appeared as the Grand Inquisitor in *Don Carlos* (Sheffield Crucible / Gielgud), the Duke of York in *Richard II* (Old Vic), Old Ekdal in *The Wild Duck* (Donmar), as James / Gore Vidal in *Terre Haute* (Assembly Rooms, Edinburgh), and as Gael in *The Cherry Orchard* (Sheffield Crucible). TV includes *Memento Mori* (BBC), *The Two Mrs Grenvilles* (Lorimar), *Friends* (Warner Bros), *Midsomer Murders* (Bentley Productions), *Don Quixote* and *Alice in Wonderland* (Hallmark), *Bertie and Elizabeth* (Carlton), *Cambridge Spies* (BBC), *Question of God* (PSB) and *Midsomer Murders X: Picture of Innocence* (Granada). Film includes: *Maurice, Let Him Have It, Orlando, Surviving Picasso, The Golden Bowl, From Hell, The Affair Of The Necklace* and *The Situation*. As director: *Bajazet* (Almeida), *Siblings* (Lyric Hammersmith) and his own version of the Flaubert - George Sand correspondence with Irene Worth, *Chere Maitre* (New York, London, Melbourne Arts Festival). Concert appearances include *Midsummer Nights Dream*, *Le Bourgeois Gentilhomme* (London Mozart Players), *A Soldiers Tale* (LSO), *Britten/Auden Theatre Pieces* (BBC singers at the Aldeburgh Festival).

HEATHER FENOUGHTY (Composer)

Heather is a multi-award winning freelance composer and sound designer. Her credits include soundtracks for several BBC primetime documentaries, two internationally recognised feature films, over 50 short films, many award-winning, most for the UK Film Council. They include one BAFTA-nominated film and two awards for Best Sound Design (48 hr Film Festival, CAN Leicester Short Film Festival). Recent theatre includes: *1139 Miles* and *Time at Moghul Gardens* (Slunglow), *Small Worlds* (MYPT) and *Shiver* (Silver Tongue). www.heather-fenoughty.com

NICK FIELDSEND (Production Manager)

Nick trained at Middlesex University. His extensive touring credits include: *Vertigo* (Red Shift), *The Reduced Shakespeare Company: Complete Works, Bible, Hollywood, Great Books and America shows all Abridged* (also Criterion), *Bottom Live*, *The Marcus Miller Jazz Band*, *The League of Gentlemen Live* (also Theatre Royal Drury Lane). Nick works in technical production for the live music industry and has worked with many internationally renowned artists.

JAMES GRIEVE (Producer)

James is co-founder and artistic director of nabokov for whom he has directed and produced: *Kitchen* (Crucible Studio, Sheffield, 2001 and Edinburgh Festival Fringe 2002); *Bedtime For Bastards* (Old Red Lion Theatre and Edinburgh Festival Fringe 2003); *Nikolina* (Edinburgh Festival Fringe 2004 and on tour 2005). As producer: *Camarilla* (Old Red Lion Theatre and Edinburgh Festival Fringe 2003); *Terre Haute* (Assembly Rooms, Edinburgh 2006). He will direct nabokov's forthcoming World Premiere production of *Artifacts* by Mike Bartlett. As a freelance director his recent credits include: *Luke Wright, Poet Laureate* (Pleasance, Edinburgh and tour), The List's Best Newcomer Award winning *Simon Brodkin : Everyone But Himself* for Avalon (Pleasance, Edinburgh), *Violent B* by Guy Jones (Jerwood Space), Aisle 16's *Poetry Boyband* (Old Red Lion – *Time Out* Critics Choice of the Year 2005) and *Comfort* by Mike Bartlett (Old Vic New Voices : Starbucks 24 Hour Plays). James trained as assistant and associate director to Josie Rourke, and on the National Theatre Studio Director's Course. He is currently Staff Director to Howard Davies on the National Theatre production of *Philistines*.

GEORGE PERRIN (Director)

George is co-founder and artistic director of nabokov. He is also Trainee Associate Director of Paines Plough and Watford Palace Theatre. He was the first recipient of the Genesis Director's Award from the Young Vic and is a member of Old Vic New Voices. As director: *Terre Haute* by Edmund White (West End; National Tour; Assembly Rooms, Edinburgh); *Camarilla* by Van Badham (Old Red Lion, London; Edinburgh Festival Fringe); *My Little Heart Dropped In Coffee* by Duncan Macmillan and *Babies* by Katie Douglas (Paines Plough/Young Vic Wild Lunch). As associate director: *Long Time Dead* by Rona Munro (Paines Plough/Drum Theatre Plymouth); *After The End* by Dennis Kelly (Paines Plough, New York; Russia; National Tour) and *Nikolina* by Van Badham (National Tour).

TARA WILKINSON (Assistant Director)

Tara trained ast LAMDA. Since graduating from the post-graduate director's course in 2006, she has assisted on the World Premiere of *Terre Haute* at the Edinburgh Festival Fringe and a workshop of a new musical by Conor Mitchell the National Theatre Studio. Whilst at LAMDA she assisted Peter James and Colin Cook, amongst others, and at The Royal Court as part of the theatre's 50th Anniversary. As director: *Unrequited* by John James Cawood (nabokov Shorts, Old Red Lion, London), an adaptation of Truman Capote's novella *Breakfast at Tiffany's*, *Ashes and Sand* by Judy Upton (Linbury Studio, LAMDA), LAMDA Duologue Showcase (Donmar Warehouse), *The Memory of Water* by Shelagh Stephenson and *Shakers* by John Godber and Jane Thornton (both Alma Tavern, Bristol and Sweet on the Royal Mile, Edinburgh Festival Fringe).

Terre Haute

Characters

James
Harrison

Scene One

Curtain up.

An urbane American, **James**, *in his early seventies – thin, balding, perfectly turned out – is standing in a spot.*

James (*to himself, as the sounds of gates opening and closing are heard*) When I arrived in Terre Haute, Indiana, this morning – the Highlands, as I like to call it – I remembered why I'd left America thirty years ago: the sheer ugliness! I thought, if I lived here I'd become a terrorist too. (*Pause.*) Then I calmed down. Whenever I become snobbish about my native land it's a sign that it's making me tense. Maybe I was just a little worried that I'd disappoint Harrison. After all, he'd written me. He'd said he liked an essay of mine about how our government is shredding the Bill of Rights. He asked me to visit him. I said that Terre Haute was a long way from Paris. He said he wanted me to write his story – to tell the world why he'd killed so many people. (*He clears his throat.*) Why did I put this on today? I didn't want to look like a lawyer, but I thought I should wear a tie – be as anonymous as possible. Little did I realise that a coat and tie would make me stand out here. I suppose I wanted to look middle class and professional to the Warden. And to Harrison, maybe a bit – well, not elegant, but as if I'd taken some pains just for him. I want him to tell me all the details of the bombing – something he's never told anyone. I want him to like me.

Lights come up on a visitors' room in prison. A clear plastic wall divides the space in half. **James** *is seated on one side at a sort of desk – he's pulling out a tape recorder and a pad and a pencil. We hear the sound of a door opening and of manacles being removed.* **Harrison**, *lean and with a light brown brush cut, comes in, shaking his wrists to get the circulation back.*

James Hello . . .

Harrison Hey . . .

An awkward silence. He sits.

How was your trip?

James   The usual air-conditioned nightmare.

Harrison   Good ol' coach – a real cattle car, right?

James   Actually, I travel first class. And on Air France you can lie down now. I'm not much good at walking any more and I have to have a wheelchair at the airport that my man pushes. I'm afraid that since I defended you on CNN I'm on a terrorist list –

Harrison   You're kidding! Fuckin' federal fascist bullshit –

James   Sadly, I'm not kidding. So I have to go to a little room and the wheelchair has to be dismantled – and if they could unscrew me they'd do so as well. (*Laughs, remembering.*) I'm afraid there was a bit of a kerfuffle when they asked me if I had packed my bag myself. Without thinking, I said, 'Of course not! My man did it – I've never packed a bag in my life.'

Harrison (*unsmiling*)   Your man . . . Oh, your butler or whatever. You know, we've exchanged so many letters but they've always been about ideas, not too personal, and here you are – in person.

James   I suppose there's something dangerous about meeting one's pen pal. In the virtual reality of correspondence there are no sagging bellies or triple chins or snobbish references to servants. Am I right or am I right?

Harrison   And when you meet him, the other guy, the prisoner, he might turn out to be too young or too dumb or too redneck or not worth the trouble –

James   When I was your age people in my crowd said, a man can never be too young or too dumb . . .

*He sees **Harrison**'s wounded expression.*

James   Sorry. Just a little joke in dubious taste.

Harrison   So. Mister. James. Brevoort. Is that how you say it? 'Brevoort'? I've been reading you so much the last three years in jail, man, but I never heard anyone say your name.

James   That's America for you. We don't exactly make our writers into celebrities. You said it right – Brevoort – though I suppose the Dutch would aspirate it or something, but that's the right American pronunciation.

Harrison   So. Mister Brevoort. I guess I never would have met you in a million years if I hadn't killed 168 men, women and children.

James   Are you kidding? I'd grab any chance to come to Terre Haute . . .

He laughs, then asks in a different voice:

How many children?

He pushes the recorder towards **Harrison**.

Harrison (*in a soft but steady voice*)   We'll get into all that later.

James (*after a long silence*)   I know what it's like to be reduced to –

Harrison (*simultaneously*)   I just feel so honoured to be here, talking to –

They both break off and laugh.

James   You first.

Harrison   Sorry. Please go ahead.

James   I was saying, by way of apology for asking you about the . . . damages . . . that I know what it's like to be reduced, commodified, turned into just one thing.

Harrison   In my case you can't really blame the press for that.

Pause.

(*Wryly.*) Can you?

James   I see your point.

Harrison   Didn't you just say, 'one's pen pal'? I never heard anyone ever say 'one' before. Maybe Sebastian Cabot said that once on TV . . .

James   Ouch.

Harrison   No offence. Maybe that's how . . . important people, rich people, the – well, the ruling class talk. Or Englishmen. What would I know? After all your grandfather was a senator, wasn't he?

James   From Oklahoma.

Harrison   You were almost a senator yourself, right? What's weird is that you're from the ruling class and yet your politics are solid as a rock.

James   That's very nice of you to notice. But I could tell from your letters you're curious about the world. I bet you've never met anyone quite like me and I certainly haven't met anyone like you.

Harrison   And here we are, chatting away like we're at some tea party and not on death row.

James (*suspicious of so much good-natured – and premature – bonhomie*)   And listening to you or looking at you, no one would suspect you killed – how many children?

Again he holds up the recorder.

Harrison   Look. (*Standing up, his jaw muscle working.*) I guess that's the problem with you living in Paris. Everyone in America knows how many kids died in that explosion. They've had six years to absorb that information. America has memorised that statistic. But if you're just now getting the word and if it's going to be a pro—

James   Of course I know how many there were. I was feeling it from your side for the first time.

Harrison (*walking away*)   Look, Jack, it's not my problem. Don't spill any tears over me. For me – well, I didn't know there was a day-care centre there, but for me the kids are just part of the collateral damage. No one blames Truman for all the kids who died at Hiroshima – most of the dead were innocent civilians. I foresaw that a lot of innocent people would die. You know the guy in the next cell is the Unabomber,

Ted Kaczynski, and he's on your side, he thinks I should have bombed the building at midnight when it was empty or gone sniping for certain big bosses of the FBI and the ATF.

James   The Unabomber is here?

Harrison (*a little jealous*)   Yeah – that turn you on?

James   Not particularly. (*Smiling.*) I'm here to write about you, not him.

Harrison   What are you smiling at?

James   We must get to work.

Harrison (*abashed*)   Anyway, I don't agree with Ted. The T-shirt I was wearing on the day of the events had a slogan from Jefferson – 'The tree of liberty must be watered from time to time with the blood of patriots and tyrants.' You see – patriots and tyrants, not just tyrants.

James   I don't think that's what Jefferson meant. You make it sound as if the defender of liberty must kill both patriots and tyrants, whereas Jefferson – Oh, let's skip it. (*Fussing with the tape recorder.*) Let's begin at the beginning, with the present. Are you afraid of dying?

Harrison   No.

James   Seriously?

Harrison   No. I've been thinking it's like when I had some really bad dental surgery done once – an impacted wisdom tooth – and they gave me some Demerol for it and I thought I'd feel it going in and I'd start getting drowsy and I'd fight giving in to it – but it was like ink being dumped in water, everything suddenly went black: there was nothing. That's the way it's going to be.

I want to die to show the world that a regular Joe like me can be the perpetrator of the biggest individual act of war on American territory. The biggest in history.

James   Hmnn . . . How will your death show that? No matter. That's what *you* think. I'm not hear to debate, just to record.

Harrison   Humane. It'll be a humane death. My 'state-assisted suicide'.

James   But still, to die . . . no more tomorrows. Total extinction. The prospect of death must be chilling –

Harrison (*irritated*)   But you must have thought about it at your age. Dying . . . Doesn't a shot of Demerol sound better than . . . cancer? Alzheimer's? Stroke? Or being paralysed?

James   Why not mention one I've already got – osteoarthrosis.

Harrison (*more compassionate*)   Is that why you have to move around in a wheelchair at the airport? Osteo – what is it? Arthritis of the bones? That must be very painful. It's great that you can write and think as clearly as you do. Do you avoid taking painkillers?

James   But we're not talking about me – damn! You're not as self-centred as the usual killer, are you?

Harrison   Have you known many?

James   I've read about them. Writers, as you must know, like to study killers – remember Truman's *In Cold Blood* and Norman's *The Executioner's Song* – and those guys they wrote about –

Harrison   – were losers. Psychopaths. Pathetic small-time crooks with long records. I was never arrested even once before. I was always top of my class in math. I was off the charts in my army entrance exams. I was one of the youngest guys in the Gulf War to be made an officer. Lieutenant. I had the Bronze Star, the Expert Rifleman's Crest, the Army Commendation Medal – all that shit.

James   The Expert . . .

He's taking notes.

Harrison   I was a good shot.

James   You're sort of a gun nut, aren't you?

Harrison   You could say I'm a Second-Amendment nut, that's the one that is just one long sentence.

James 'A well regulated Militia, being necessary to the security of a free State, the right of the people to keep and bear Arms, shall not be infringed.'

Harrison I guess you don't take painkillers.

James You know I was in the army. World War II. I fought in the liberation of Italy. Pretty grisly. A whole hungry nation of people denouncing each other, killing each other . . . I had a great friend who died in the war. I don't usually bring up Bud, but – well, he was the great . . . intimacy of my life. And you remind me of him. Oh, not exactly – he was a prep-school boy, a golden boy.

Harrison (*cradling the back of his head with his hands – a little proud of his humble origins*) And I sure as hell am not. That's for dang sure. You can hear the mall in the way I talk. My family are good people, but common as dirt.

Pause.

Why are you interested in me?

James CNN came to Paris to interview me about you, right after the bombing.

Harrison I heard about that . . .

James It was an 'in-depth interview', that is, two whole minutes. And when I said on air that it was no accident that the explosion took place exactly two years to the day after Janet Reno, the Attorney General, killed eighty-one men, women and children in Waco, Texas, the interviewer rolled his eyes and I was cut off and the announcer said the international line had collapsed, but the sound engineer beside me looked at me and shook his head and he said, 'It didn't break down, they just cut you off.'

He stands a bit stiffly.

For me it's a censorship matter, first of all.

Harrison And second of all?

James   No one wants to admit that you, as a single outraged individual, were responding to a government that engineered the deaths of Allende and Lumumba, that has unsuccessfully tried to assassinate Castro and Gaddafi for years and years. Nobody wants to talk about our wars in Kosovo and Korea or Central America or Mozambique or Kenya. We are in a state of permanent war.

Harrison   I hear you, brother . . . Don't forget gun control. Don't forget Ruby Ridge, Idaho. There was Randy Weaver living peacefully with his family in a remote cabin and the FBI wanted Randy to inform on his fellow white separatists. When he refused, the FBI surrounded the cabin and on the first day shot his fourteen-year-old son and on the next day shot his wife . . .

James   And the fact that thirty million Americans are now kept under electronic surveillance or that four hundred million telephone conversations a year are monitored.

Pause.

Am I preaching to the converted?

Harrison (*smiling*)   Pretty much. But it sounds good. I'm with you. I'm glad you said all that just now; when you first came in you seemed just like one more tough reporter, determined to get your story. (*Smiling.*) When you get going like that it reminds me of that day when I read your article about the Bill of Rights. And then when I wrote you and I started getting letters from you – this sounds weird, but they meant more to me than all the perfumed letters from women I get, women who want me to send them my sperm. (*Unconsciously pressing his legs together.*) I wouldn't have guessed there'd be so many women in the world who want to carry my sperm. (*More serious.*) Are you interested in me and my story or in my form of protest? You don't really want to write my biography, do you?

James   No, that's just something I told the Warden to get in. I'm going to write a series of articles about you in *The Nation*. How do you feel about that?

Harrison   A biography would be a waste of your time. I'm not sure you should be looking up high school transcripts and parents' birthdates –

James   This late in the day, you mean? You think I might be too old to write a biography? A little long in the tooth to eat such a big meal.

Harrison   I'm not making any references to your age. I never thought about your age until your wrote me on a typewriter. I looked at those black ink perforations in the paper – it could have been Braille as far as I was concerned. No, I mean you're a great thinker. You've known everyone – the Kennedys, James Baldwin, Truman Capote . . .

James   Sadly, I can't say that some day when you're older you'll see that past experiences count for nothing. You're not going to have a future. But take it from me, no one lives off his memories. Just as no one is full today because he ate a good meal yesterday. I may have met lots of interesting people in the past but that doesn't bring me much satisfaction now. I need a project today – I'll need another one tomorrow. You're today's project.

Harrison   The funny thing is that I was afraid of disappointing you. Of not being smart enough. Of not knowing enough about the issues that interest you. Maybe of not being interested in the same issues.

James   That's odd – I was afraid of disappointing you, too.

Harrison (*laughing*)   It's sort of like a first date.

James   I must seem like a grandfather to you.

Harrison   My grandfather was the only man I ever loved.

There is the loud sound of a buzzer. He stands.

That's it – time's up. They just give us twenty minutes, though sometimes the guard goes off for a coffee break and forgets. I guess they don't want us to work up an escape plan – or get to like each other. (*Gently.*) Till *mañana* – sleep well, you hear?

We hear the gate being opened and the sound of manacles being attached to **Harrison**'s *wrists and ankles. The lights dim.*

James (*in a spot*)   Are all sociopaths so charming? So clever at appealing to an old man's vanity? He certainly has his flirtatious side, if someone so correct and military can be said to be a flirt.

Pause.

He even said we were on a first date.

Scene Two

James *is seated. We hear the gate opening.* **Harrison** *comes in. Does a bit of stretching-out exercising – twisting to right and left, crouching, standing, touching his toes, adjusting his neck and head with both hands.*

Harrison (*simultaneously*) Did you sleep well? Sweet dreams?

James I always sleep well. I leave nothing to chance. I've taken a ten-milligram Valium every night of my life. And you?

Harrison I had long weird-ass dreams about going places. In one of them my grandfather and I were going to sail on the *Queen Mary* across the Atlantic – can you still do that?

James No.

Harrison And we couldn't find our seats. No one would help us. I thought I'd rented us a nice cabin, but when we found our place it was just a bench where people were coming and going. Everything was old and falling apart. I guess I was just happy to see my grandfather alive and well again, though I felt I'd disappointed him with our seats.

Sits down, looks expectantly at **James**.

James (*shaking the end of a pencil at him as if he's in pursuit of an elusive thought*) I've been thinking. We have to protect the American Republic from the American Empire. That's what you were doing –

Harrison Hold on! I have my own reasons for doing what I did.

Pause.

I've been thinking too. I'm the one who's got to die in three days. I'm the one who did just one big thing in my short life –

James And I've done nothing? Is that what you're saying?

Harrison (*gathers his thoughts*) The only reason that could justify me killing so many people and losing my own life now is getting my message out. And you're the only one who can do that. Without you, I'm just one more American monster,

Jeffrey Dahmer eating all those poor guys, freezing them and then eating them 'cause the problem with living guys, he said, is that they leave you, you end up alone. Or I'll be some asshole up in a Texas tower gunning down co-eds, or a weirdo killing nurses in Florida because he can't get a date on Saturday night. One more sick fuck in this big lonely country.

James   OK. Let's make a bargain – I'll defend you in print if you tell me now what you've never told anyone – the story of how you blew up the Murrah Building.

Harrison   You drive a tough bargain. But I've learned in here that information is my only form of property. I'm not ready to play my best card.

James   OK. Tell me anything. Even things I don't like.

Harrison   Like what? What don't you like?

James   Racism. Anti-Semitism.

Harrison   OK, OK. I'm no racist. I joined the KKK for about three minutes after the war because their handouts made them sound like they were against big government and gun control. But they're not. They're just against blacks, that's all, and that doesn't interest me.

James   I'm not sure I believe you. What about –

Harrison   I wore their 'White Power' sweatshirt for a while around the army base, but that was just because I was sick of the black soldiers and their 'Black Power' shirts. That's a kind of racism, too. What I like are disciplined, patriotic people, honest and straightforward, whether they're Jewish or Christian, black or white –

James   Male or female? We haven't even mentioned sex yet and if I'm going to write about you, your sexual quirks have to be the cornerstone in the Land of Freud. I suppose I could hand out to you the usual talk-show checklist – child abuse? Abuse *of* children? Abuse *while* a child? Incest?

Harrison   That stuff disgusts me.

James   Prolonged chastity?

Pause, then, more seriously:

Did you ever sleep with anyone? A woman? Or with a man?

Harrison   A man! Christ . . . I'm not gay. (*Catching himself.*) Not that I've got anything against gays – I just don't know anything about – I mean, it's not part of my . . . And I wouldn't want a gay guy to hit on me.

James   Although I've been a practising bisexual for half a century, I can't say I understand anything more about sexuality now than that day I started out, so long ago . . .

Harrison   Bisexual . . . I can't really imagine that.

James   Why not?

Harrison   I just can't picture – Well, I've been in the barracks and in prison –

James   But always in isolation in prison, right?

Harrison   True . . . But no matter where I was or under what condition, I just can't imagine –

James   Is that why you welcomed the death penalty? Were you afraid you'd be made into some brute's bitch? You're a pretty guy, after all.

Harrison   They'd be more likely to off me as a child-killer. (*A delayed response.*) Pretty? Fuck . . . Anyway, I'd join the right gang, defend myself –

James   So you've been thinking about it? Can you imagine having sex with anyone? – I just say that because a lot of the men who can't imagine having sex with another man are virgins –

Harrison (*a bit irritated*)   Of course I can picture – with a woman – I've had – it's just that girls, well, of course I like them, but they've been on the margins – I've had an event-packed life . . .

Look, I think we should get off the subject of sex.

James   It's not even one of my subjects. You've read me –
you know.

Harrison (*tapping the plastic partition*)   In the time I've got to
live, I mean sex – (*laughs*) this is going to make sure I don't get
to touch anyone . . . Promise you won't write about me and
sex. (*Laughs.*) And DON'T SAY I'M PRETTY. Christ . . .

I've gotten weak and out of shape here at Terre Haute.

Pause.

Are you going to stay?

James   Stay?

Harrison   For the execution?

James   Do you want me to?

Harrison (*after a struggle*)   Yes.

James   Why?

Harrison   You'll be my only . . . witness. My sister isn't
coming. My dad neither. I didn't want them to go through all
that.

James   I'll be there.

Turning on the tape recorder.

How do you feel about your father? His testimony, after all,
was pretty damaging.

Harrison   The poor guy. He knew nothing about Oklahoma
– he hadn't even watched it on TV. And then all of a sudden
there were all these FBI goons in his living room grilling him.
He's a good law-abiding citizen, an auto-worker – he's always
said and done the right thing. He's the kind of guy you can't
really feel . . . close to, but you gotta hand it to him, he's led a
good solid life. I guess he admitted to the government agents
that I'd gotten pretty worked up over Waco and that whenever
Clinton or Janet Reno were mentioned on TV I'd go ballistic.

Pause.

Poor Dad. The FBI flew him out to see me and ordered him to ask me all these questions, but I wouldn't answer him.

I hated doing that, giving him the silent treatment like that, but my lawyers had told me not to talk to anyone. He just looked so bewildered. Finally I said to him, 'Dad, you better go home,' and he just shuffled out.

James   What about your sister?

Harrison   She's a feisty little thing. (*Smiling.*) She loves jello-wrestling at a country western bar in Niagra Falls.

I love my sister. You could say she's the witness to my life. I didn't want to involve her in the events of April 1995 –

James   The bombing, you mean?

Harrison   I prefer to call it 'the events'. More neutral. More objective.

James   Sounds French – *les événements*. OK – so you didn't want to involve her . . .

Harrison   But I did without meaning to. I kept mailing her pages from *The Turner Diaries*, this really cool novel I read –

James   Right-wing trash.

Harrison   What'd you say?

James   *The Turner Diaries*? That racist white-supremacist right-wing garbage? All about a people's revolution against Jews and blacks in which the 'people' are defined as white gun-hobbyists? There's a scene in which blacks are confined in a ghetto in San Francisco of all places –

Harrison   It's my favourite book.

James   *The Turner Diaries* may be pro-gun and anti-government, but it's also full of foolishness. It claims the United States and the United Nations are joining forces to imprison our own people.

Harrison   But that's already happening. The government is building concentration camps where they can imprison all rebels and dissenters – millions of cells have already been built.

James (*turning off the tape recorder*)   You really do have a screw loose. The tragedy of your life is that you didn't go to college.

Harrison   My life ain't tragic, man.

James   Oh? I'd say it's almost Aristotelian in its tragic purity. And your tragic flaw is that you're highly intelligent but you were never properly stimulated intellectually, and you ended up reading all these paranoid scenarios . . .

Harrison (*after a long silence*)   It must be nice to be able to pigeonhole other folks. At an age when other men are drooling on themselves down Florida way, you're sitting off in elegant Paris in your elegant suit, cool as a cucumber, if that's the right bisexual vegetable . . .

James (*softly, a bit repentant*)   Sorry.

Harrison   What the hell you mean, never properly fuckin' stimulated?

James   Intellectually. I was talking about intellectual under-stimulation.

Harrison   Listen, I read a lot –

James   I dare say you really are a first-rate mind but you were so damn arrogant you thought you didn't need to go on to higher studies. Mary McCarthy once wrote a very funny essay about meeting an army officer who was an anti-Semite, and she realised that anti-Semitism was his only form of intellectual life, and to take his anti-Semitism away from him would be like stripping the ancient Greeks of the syllogism.

Harrison   Now you're rambling. Showing your age, James. I don't know who Mary Whatsit is, but I'll tell you one thing: what I liked about *The Turner Diaries* is that it told me how to make a big bomb.

James   Is that where you got the recipe for your bomb? Tell me about that.

Harrison   Why should I trust you to tell it the right way – *my* way?

James   *We're in this together.* You know that I've received several bushels of hate mail because I wrote that piece saying people should take you seriously.

Harrison   But for you it's something exciting and forbidden you can dabble with and then move on – not for me.

James   We're wasting time.

Harrison   You think I'm stupid.

James   I'm not like all those people who call you 'a useful idiot'.

Harrison   What the hell? Who calls me that?

James   There are people who think the FBI set you up. That they infiltrated some militia groups who in turn pushed you into bombing the Murrah Building.

Harrison   I never got instructions from anyone. I acted alone. And what would have been the FBI's motive?

James   There's a retired army officer who's going around saying he examined the ruins and that he determined that there were seventeen bombs within the building placed there by the FBI. But you, like a dumb duck, thought you created all that damage all by yourself. Their motive? By pushing the useful idiot into taking the rap for making a huge doo-doo, President Clinton had a good pretext for passing the Anti-Terrorist Bill, which gave him as the president even more tyrannical powers.

Harrison (*ironically*)   Hey, James, I'm really happy you told me all that fuckin' crap! (*Hitting the table.*) I don't know which part of what you just said makes me madder – that people think I was a stooge for the FBI or that the events only gave the government an excuse for extending its tyranny . . .

(*Anguished.*) Fuck! It's like I not only have to die for my so-called crimes, I have to also prove I did them. How fucked up is that?

James   It is fairly absurd. But did you act alone? How can I set the record straight if you won't confide in me?

Harrison   But you don't believe this . . . this conspiracy theory, do you? Tell me you don't. Tell me you won't even put it into words, because once people hear some twisted shit like that – James, promise!

James *is icily silent.*

Harrison   OK, OK. You're a writer. I believe in freedom of speech, right? You gotta call 'em the way you see 'em. (*Suspicious.*) Do you think I'm dumb?

James   Intelligence doesn't mean memorising lots of information or using big words. It means quickly changing contexts and seeing everything from the long shot of tragedy or then the close-up of comedy.

Harrison   I'm not sure I see myself as a big comedy.

James   Intelligence means seeing oneself in a satirical light or even a literary light – as when you said that we were at a tea party and not on death row. Intelligence means seeing yourself as a character. That's the way my friend Bud was intelligent. He could pick up on anything. He was always laughing because he could see the irony in almost any situation. He wasn't smart in any other way – he never got all the way through a book.

Harrison   I've gotten through lots of books. Maybe I'm not really like your golden boy. Are you still going to write about me?

James (*turning the recorder back on*)   I want you to tell me about the big turning points in your thinking, the moments that led you to the Events.

Harrison   The Gulf War was pretty big. I had always been a crack soldier, but after the war I tried to get into the Special

Forces, the Green Berets, but I fucked up. I wasn't even twenty-three yet. The fuckin' war had fucked me up.

James   So you'd been a big success in the army and then suddenly you failed, you were a failure, you were failing –

Harrison   You sound like a stuck needle. (*Mocking him.*) 'Failed', 'failure', 'failing' . . . (*Exploding*) Yeah, I felt shitty. Satisfied?

James   Highly. I'm highly satisfied. (*In a low voice.*) You're lucky it's me writing about you. One of the usual cornball pathographers would have seized on to your rejection by the Green Berets as the motive for the bombing.

Harrison   That's too fucked up even to think about.

James   Any more turning points?

Harrison (*pulling himself together*)   Let's talk about Waco. The Events in Oklahoma City took place on April 19, 1995, exactly two years after Waco. As you said on TV. I guess I was psyched for Waco anyway, since I was trying to make a living in construction down in Florida – a state I'd chosen because it doesn't have income taxes – and then I get this letter from the army and it goes, 'You owe us $1,058 because we fucked up and overpaid you and we demand full restitution.' Here I am, trying to get away from big government, I'm broke and I'm still feeling the effects of their Gulf War. I wrote a shit-kickin' letter telling them to seize my car since it was the only fuckin' thing of value I owned. I thought, hell, I'll go on welfare and bleed the system dry.

Pause.

A week later I was in Waco.

James   Why are all the rebels in this country either gun-nuts or Christ-nuts?

Harrison   Because those are the two groups who care about their freedom passionately enough to defend it. The rest of the country is zoning out in front of their TVs.

Waco was a rallying point for all us anti-government guys. I'd
met a lot of militia guys when I was travelling around the country
going to gun shows. I went to about eighty gun shows, buying
and selling rifles and explosive caps. We were all there in Waco
because the Bureau of Alcohol, Tobacco and Firearms had
staged an illegal raid on the Branch Davidians. The government
said the Davidians were stockpiling weapons – what you and
I would call collecting guns. There'd been a shoot-out and
four ATF agents died and six Davidians. There were lots of
Davidian wounded too – including Koresh the leader.

Then the FBI was called in and they put on the heat. No press.
They wouldn't let reporters close to the compound. Day and
night they turned on floodlights around the compound and
played Nancy Sinatra's 'These Boots Are Made for Walking'.

He sings a few bars.

James   That would clearly induce a psychotic break in
anyone . . .

Harrison   And they spliced in the screech of dying rabbits . . .

James   Funny, I always thought the screeching was part of
the original recording. How long did you stay?

Harrison   Two days. I couldn't take it.

James   Then you cleared out?

Harrison   I had a run-in with the Feds.

James   Really? I never heard about that, and I pride myself
on having read every scrap of information about you that
exists.

Harrison (*flattered*)   I don't think it got into the press.
(*Serious again.*) I was driving right toward the compound – you
remember, it was called Mount Carmel – and I was about
three miles from Mount Carmel and six agents stopped me –
I could see about another eight or nine standing off a-ways,
fully armed. They said, 'Where are you going?' (*Getting louder
and more violent.*) I said, 'I'm on a public road and I'm heading
for Mount Carmel.' They asked me if I was a member of the

press. I said no, and they told me to turn around and clear out.
My old army training in the Gulf War came back to me – I
felt that kind of excitement. I wondered if I started throwing
grenades and shooting if I couldn't take them all out. My
blood was beating so loud in my ears I was afraid they'd hear it.
My whole body was tense, every muscle in my legs and arms
and shoulders was coiled tight as a spring, I wanted to go
ballistic like in Iraq, but this time against the real enemy, the
FBI –

James   You don't need to talk so loud.

Harrison   Are you worried they'll hear me? They've heard
it all before –

James   No, your voice hurts my ears. It starts resonating. It's
relentless.

Harrison   Sorry . . . (*Decides to make it all a joke.*) Want me to
sing 'These Boots Are Made for Walking'? I can get you really
squirming . . .

James   Sorry. I don't know why my nerves are so . . . easily
triggered. It scares me a bit when you start shouting about
taking them all out.

Harrison   Well, I am a mass murderer, remember?

Pause.

There are so many people eager to see me die. They're going
to transmit my death agonies direct to a room in Oklahoma
where the victims' families can watch. I don't know if you
noticed that a couple months back when I was transferred here
to Terre Haute I was a lot heavier? I'd bulked up because I was
afraid that someone might try to assassinate me during the
transfer – I wanted some fat on me to insulate me. There were
dozens of people gathered around waiting for me to come out
of the prison yard. When they saw me they booed. Coming
back from the Gulf I was applauded as a war hero and here
I was being booed – for almost the same thing: killing people.

There – am I talking in a more normal voice now?

The buzzer sounds. We hear the gates opening. **Harrison** *steps out and is shackled.* **James** *steps forward, supported by his cane, and addresses the audience.*

James   Why did I tell him about Bud? I thought I was in charge – destabilising him, asking him questions about his sex life, getting him to talk about his grandfather, maybe even vaguely playing his grandfather to him. Oh, I've been full of my usual tricky interviewing techniques. I like switching back and forth from affection to nastiness, from playing the indulgent parent to the harsh punishing father. I made fun of him for failing to get into the Green Berets. I humiliated him for his stupidity in embracing *The Turner Diaries* – and then I praised his intelligence. Just my usual techniques for breaking down his resistance.

But to keep talking about Bud, about myself . . . (*Starting over.*) Tonight I came back to my Larry Bird motel room and I listened to my tapes, not because I was preparing new questions for tomorrow, but because I liked the sound of his voice – his maddening, loud, impossible voice. I put on the earphones, not because I was afraid of disturbing the neighbours but because I liked that voice booming right inside me.

Scene Three

Harrison *comes back into the room, unshackled.*

James The guards still aren't very welcoming. I still haven't had a hello from any of them.

Harrison I don't have a quarrel with the personnel here. They're just doing their jobs and being badly paid for it. (*Reflecting.*) I want to maintain a military . . . decorum. Is that the right word? I think it helps me project my message if in prison I behave in a perfect, a good, strong way.

Am I talking too loud?

James Did I hurt your feelings with that remark of mine?

Harrison No – well, maybe. (*More definite.*) Yes.

James Isn't that strange – you can hurt a mass murderer's feelings by telling him he's talking too loud. Norman Mailer said that you can tell a stranger over dinner that you're sure he wants to sleep with his mother and he'll just smile, flattered, but he'll hate you for life if you suggest he's using the wrong fork.

Harrison *doesn't laugh but just stares at him.*

James Well, we should get to work.

Harrison Mass murderer, huh? Is that going to be your title? I wonder how that will play with the parish back home.

James You're not a believer, are you?

Harrison I'm going to have the last rites.

James Whatever for?

Harrison For my parents' sake. I was brought up Catholic, though it was more the bingo-and-basketball kind of Catholicism. Nothing too heavy.

James A little grope-in-the-confessional-booth kind of Catholicism?

Harrison (*ignoring the innuendo*)   And my parents, they're divorced – which isn't too Catholic, either. But don't make too much out of that. Half the people in America have divorced parents.

James   I am more interested in your ideas than in your life. Most Americans think you blew up that building out of innate madness or unmotivated, Iago-like evil. I can't hope to make you sympathetic to the public, but I do want to make you credible.

Harrison   Why do you care about all this? You don't even live here.

James   I am an American. I care about what happens to this country, which is a way of saying I care about what happens to the world. Anyway, it's my role. The gadfly of the nation.

Harrison   Well, Mr Gadfly, what do you believe about the Davidians?

James   I believe they were a strange group expecting the end of the world –

Harrison   There they were right on the money.

James   I think Koresh probably was shtupping those fourteen-year-old girls, but with their parents' consent.

Harrison (*unamused*)   Even if it was child-abuse, that's a matter for the local sheriff, not for an army of federal agents in military helicopters armed with machine guns.

James   I also know that the FBI convinced Janet Reno to leave her headquarters in Washington in order to give a speech somewhere, and while she was out of the office they breached the walls of the compound, flooded the rooms with an inflammable gas and ignited it by firing caps into the building at two strategic points.

Harrison   I believe you, but do you have any proof?

James   Absolutely. There was a heat-sensitive surveillance film of the compound shot from a plane –

Harrison There was? A Flir photo? Forward-looking infrared?

James It shows two streaks entering the compound and the fire breaking out a minute later. During the congressional hearing the FBI said those were reflections off a mirror or a bottle cap, but a Flir photo doesn't register light, only heat –

Harrison (*agreeing*) It captures only heat . . . no light bouncing off an object.

James The FBI ignited the gas and created two fireballs that rolled through the whole compound and burned all the inhabitants alive. When a few tried to escape through the roof they were gunned down. The Flir film caught all that, too – I can show you the charts and film clips . . . (*Catching himself.*) Well, maybe not in this place. You'll have to take my word for it.

Harrison (*after a pause*) You couldn't have given me a better gift.

James Gift? How so?

Harrison Because that proves those folks didn't commit suicide. That the ATF assaulted them illegally and the FBI murdered them –

James But there's still the little matter that they were manufacturing illegal firearms.

Harrison That was never proved. But if it was true, then they should have been tried and convicted, and the conviction could have been appealed, but at Waco the people were executed without a trial.

Pause.

No, that's your gift – proof that it was government-sanctioned killing. I feel justified in what I did.

James Well, if you ever want to give me a gift –

Harrison I know, I know. Well, don't think I've forgotten what you want.

James (*lost in his own thoughts*)   What a waste.

Harrison   What are you talking about? The Davidians?

James   No. You. It seems unthinkable you're going to be dead so soon. I'm not proposing an argument for changing your punishment; I'm just saying I think it's a shame you have to die. A shame . . . for me.

Harrison   For you? Why should my death matter to you?

James   If you knew me better, you'd understand.

Harrison   But I don't know anything about you. I didn't read your autobiography − I couldn't get it here in prison. I know nothing about your past −

James   Which in any case is banal − murderously cold father, seductive mother, Choate, Yale, flirtation with Hollywood, flirtation with politics, funny essays, not-so-funny novels, not too much love, lots of sex.

Harrison   Wow! That's crazy the way you can just rattle your whole life off like that. A little scary, too.

James   Why scary?

Harrison   You treat yourself like a −

James   Like a character in a novel?

Harrison   Like a thing. You treat yourself like a . . . thing. I want to know about your life now.

James (*disconcerted*)   Why?

Harrison   How else do two people become friends? For me it's now or never. Instant or it ain't happenin'. Don't you want to be friends?

James (*startled*)   Of course I want to be friends. My life now? I think my life is a little bleak. I'm not really up to much writing now − the only things of interest I've written in the last two years are these essays about you. I'm glad to see they've stirred up the shit: I like to be controversial.

Harrison   Me too.

James   Decidedly.

Harrison   You crack me up, dude: 'decidedly'. Never in a million years could I predict what you're going to say next.

James (*smiling*)   I've always been the most productive writer of my generation. I'm not saying the best, but certainly the most productive. But now that I can only write in spurts on days when I'm feeling well enough, I have whole great hectares of time to fill . . .

Harrison   Heck . . . ?

James   Hectares. Two and a half acres. You don't know the metric system?

Harrison   We don't use it in this country.

James   Quite. Usually I stay in bed and read in the mornings. I have a nice English girl, Margaret, who works for me. Her job is to read all my friends' books and write plot summaries so that I can dash off letters of congratulation without interrupting my real reading. You know I write historical novels, and they require tremendous research, which I love.

Harrison   And in the afternoons?

James   I might get out and see an art exhibit – oh, people who live in big cities always lie and say that, but they only go to a museum once a year at best. I don't know. I've been depressed.

Harrison   Why are you depressed?

James   Old age. Boredom. Disappointment. Paris weather is pretty depressing – it rains every day in the winter.

Harrison   And sex?

James (*looks uncomfortable*)   Get it! Now you're in the hot seat. What I like about you is that you really are blind to age. No other young man would ask a seventy-one-year-old about his sex life.

Harrison   Pretty cool way to avoid answering.

James   Fair enough. Well, I have a sex life. I always have.
I pay for it. I always have.

Harrison   You've always paid for it? Why? Or is that what
gay guys do?

James   Oh, no, most gay men are frightfully vain and stingy:
'Who, me, pay? I, who am a beauty in my own right?' I always
got it out of the way in the afternoon. In the evening all my
friends, the people I dine with in restaurants, are always
cruising the whole night, eyeing some mediocre middle-aged
freebie with bad teeth, whereas I am invariably the soul of
attentiveness toward my friends because I've already –

Harrison   Gotten it out of the way?

James   Does that sound cold-blooded to you?

Harrison   I don't know.

James   I'm sure you're in there somewhere behind those
unreadable eyes judging me.

Harrison   I'm judging you?

James   Do you think I'm cold and self-centred? Heartless?
People your age aren't supposed to know all the horrors of
senile sex lives – it would make you too cynical to want to go
on . . .

Harrison   But I'm not going on, remember? You might as
well tell me the whole truth and nothing but the truth.

James   Do you find my life pathetic?

Harrison   Do you?

James   Dull. Elegant and dull. An elegant ritual. A dullness
punctuated with anxiety, since it can only end in sickness and
pain and death . . .

Harrison   Are you afraid of dying?

James   Yes. We're both on death row.

Harrison   But you must be proud of your accomplishments.

James   Yes. Yes, I am. Are you?

Harrison   What I did had to be done. The tree of liberty had to watered with blood. That should have been clear to everyone.

James   But it wasn't: nobody knows your motives. At first everyone assumed you were an Arab terrorist, then they saw you as a madman. Then they said you were a dupe of other forces.

Harrison   That's where you come in.

James (*putting in a new tape*)   You seem like you were the average American kid until you went off to the Gulf War.

Harrison   I was pretty damn average. I'm not sure I can reel it off as fast you did about your life, but I'll give it a try: I was born in 1968 –

James   A revolutionary year throughout the world.

Harrison   It took a long time before I found out about that – news of that sort doesn't travel fast in upstate New York. (*Concentrates.*) I grew up in a three-bedroom ranch. A kid sister. I got everyone to play – cops and robbers and cowboys and Indians. I was always the good guy – the sheriff.

James (*taking notes*)   The good guy . . .

Harrison   Or we'd tape flashlights to plastic golf clubs and have *Star Wars* duels. Of course I was always Luke Skywalker.

James   The blond.

Harrison   Yeah. I was a little guy, too small for sports, though strangely enough I was pretty good at basketball in eighth grade.

James   But later you filled out nicely. I see boys like you wandering around New York with their parents, farm boys on a family outing to New York, taking in a musical, their blond eyebrows sun-bleached, their eyes empty – young, dumb and

full of come. That's what we used to say. Zoning out with
their parents – thinking about girls. Or guns. You've made me
realise they're probably thinking about guns.

Pause.

Harrison   Do you have the hots for me?

James   I always go for the unobtainable.

Taps the plastic wall.

I haven't exactly said I have the hots for you. That's something
you've dreamed up. I'm just talking about your looks. I know
you have a highly original mind. Your looks are so . . . banal
that they excite me. You look like all those blank-eyed West
Point cadets.

Harrison   O . . . K.

James   You have the look of someone permanently at
attention. Ready to take orders though in your heart you want
to give them.

I wonder what sort or orders you would give?

Harrison *doesn't respond. He paces his cell.*

James (*after an uncomfortable moment*)   You finished high school?

Harrison   Yeah, and then I went to computer school for a
short while, but when they suddenly added academic subjects
I felt bored and dropped out. I went to work at Burger King
and started reading gun magazines and books about
survivalism. I became a survivalist. I put gallons of water in
the basement and canned food and a whole arsenal. I read
The Turner Diaries and suddenly I saw we were about to be
invaded.

James   By whom?

Harrison   The New World Order.

James   What's that?

Harrison (*outraged*)   'What's that'?! You're an educated man
and you could ask me 'What's that?' You're shittin' me, right?

James I honestly don't know what it is.

Harrison You're either dangerously ignorant or part of the conspiracy or pretending not to know just to rile me – good interviewing technique, James.

James I'd appreciate a straightforward answer rather than all this speculation about my motives.

Harrison Everyone – well, practically everyone – knows what the New World Order is. It's the organisation that's made up of the FBI and the Earth First! terrorists and David Rockefeller and the other Marxist leaders on the Council of Foreign Relations –

James What's this!? You think that nice, mild, philanthropic David Rockefeller is a *Marxist*, whatever that means after the fall of Communism?

Harrison Of course he is – and then there's the Trilateral Commission and the eight Jewish bankers who run the Federal Reserve, all acting under the orders of the United Nations to conquer this country and all others and establish a one-world tyranny.

James First of all, no huge conspiracy theory like that ever makes sense, given how lazy and gossipy and disorganised politicians are – you can't even get two senators from Alabama to agree to do lunch much less arrange for the entire penniless United Nations to get together to invade this country –

Harrison Well, you're pretty damn sure of yourself, but I've studied this shit: soon there will be a single worldwide police force and a single currency. A civil war is coming down the pike, sure as shit. They've already taken away our right to use semi-automatic weapons.

James I'm stupefied.

Harrison By what?

James The revelation of your ignorance.

Harrison Well, fuck you too.

James   Your 'philosophy', as lowbrows like you call their
opinions – your 'philosophy of life'. It's just a ragbag of
enemies you and your buddies have thrown together out of
a total ignorance of history.

Harrison   Not everyone went to Yale.

James   I can't believe how stupid you are. But what really
disturbs me is that I've made myself stupid.

Harrison   By having the hots for me?

James   Yes, you put your finger on it.

Harrison   By taking me more seriously than I deserve? Are
you afraid you hitched your big Rolls-Royce to the wrong star?

James   Thank you for opening my eyes. What I haven't
brought up because I've been so besotted by you is the violence
you created and the lives you took. What about all the people
you killed?

Harrison   I won't listen to this shit. I thought you'd be above
this sentimental horseshit about the lives I took. I learned the
value of life from my government – from what the Feds did in
Iraq and Ruby Ridge and Waco.

James   I'm an atheist and you're not much of a believer, but
all we have, each one of us, is our story. The story of our life.
It's the novel we're writing by just existing, and you shredded
all those lines and chapters and books, you burned the books
of their lives in one big bonfire – and it wasn't your right to do
that!

Harrison   You're making me sick – soon you'll be talking
about the sacredness of life.

James   It *is* sacred! Even an atheist must act *as if* it's sacred
because if it's not, then someone like you or Jeffrey Dahmer or
George W. Bush can just terminate lives when he feels like it.
Look at what you did – all those mangled bleeding bodies of
children, those people armless and legless or decapitated by
falling girders, no lethal injections for them, no humane death.

Harrison (*mimicking playing the violin*)   You're breaking my heart.

James   Not one moment of remorse on your part. Not one word of regret. Your stupid principles have blinded you to the most basic thing of all – all those burning books of lives are sacred books, they cannot be dismissed as 'collateral damage'.

Harrison (*coldly*)   Get the fuck out.

James   Oh, come now –

Harrison (*in a rage, throwing himself against the plastic barrier*) I said get the fuck out now or I'll melt my way through this plastic and strangle your ugly old wobbly neck, you fuckin' arrogant asshole. I'll kill you, old man. I'm the one who was fooled – I thought you were the solution, but you ain't nothin' but more of the problem. You're just one more Socialist wannabe slave, one more bleeding-heart humanist cooing pigeon. I've got to wait for the guards but you can leave on your own. (*In a low voice.*) That's an order. You wanted an order.

James (*bangs on the door*)   Hello! Hello! Get me out of here! Guard! I want out! Guard!

Harrison   You pathetic old bastard. I feel sorry for the poor jerks who are so broke they have to stick their dicks down your sorry old gullet.

James   Hello! Let me out of here!

*They are both waiting to be released. Here the time might stretch on fairly long before **Harrison** is shackled and led away and then **James** is released. In the waiting period **Harrison** and **James** keep glancing at each other, angrily, then sheepishly. This is an agonising moment.*

*The lights gradually fade and **James** is picked out in just a pool of light, which is also gradually fading.*

James   I rushed back to my motel and changed my reservations – I'm afraid I rather shouted at the woman when she said it was too late to get me on a plane right away. Then I said I might as well wait a day and leave not the next morning but the morning after. Why? What did I hope to see in Terre Haute?

I went to visit the Eugene V. Debs museum, his lower-middle-class family home, preserved exactly as it had been when he was born in Terre Haute. It was very clean and very sad. But I was glad I'd seen it at least once in this lifetime – after all, he stood as the Socialist candidate for President six times. The decency of his life and house comforted me.

I got back into my room and fell into a deep sleep. I was awakened when the Warden phoned me to say that the prisoner would like to see me. Tomorrow. For twenty minutes at ten o'clock. Of course I'll be there.

Thank you.

The lights are almost extinguished.

Scene Four

Lights come flooding back in a cold daylight. We're in the cell and **James** *is standing in a corner when* **Harrison** *enters.* **James** *and* **Harrison** *look at each other furtively and then begin to speak at once.*

James   I'm terribly sorry that –

Harrison (*same time*)   Hey, I don't know what – (*Interrupts himself.*) Go ahead.

James   You first.

Harrison   I have something to tell you. I'm glad you were willing to come back.

James   You seem much calmer.

Harrison (*cool, passionless, almost as if he's meditating*)   I can't afford to be so . . . (*Can't think of the word.*) So . . . busy now. I'll be executed tomorrow and I want to be cool and collected. Not just to impress everyone, but really. Really cool. I want to settle all my emotional accounts. It's very important that I face death like a soldier.

James (*looking up*)   Everybody agrees that you went through everything like a soldier – the arrest, the transfers from one prison to another, though the crowd was howling for your blood, the trial.

Harrison   I owe it to my cause. Otherwise I look as if I was crazy or had lost my convictions. I want to be like the . . . well the kamikaze pilots. I'm sure they were shitting a brick but they made the sacrifice to their emperor.

James   Is there anything I can do to help you?

Harrison   All I care about is your words – what you're going to say about me. I guess you are going to show me as a heartless murderer – well, so be it. But don't skip over all the other things we've talked about. You said we're each a book waiting to be written; well, you're writing mine, the story of my life, even if it's only a few articles.

James   I'm going to defend you – which isn't going to be easy. But I'm a big boy: I'm up to it.

Harrison (*laughing*)   You sure as hell are!

We don't have much time left. I've made a decision. I want to tell you about the actual bombing.

Where should I begin?

James   Tell me about the bomb itself.

Harrison   I rented a big Ryder truck and drove it on the morning of the day before the Events to a storage area where I'd collected all my material. It was an isolated spot so no one would see me loading the truck with a hundred and eight bags of ammonium nitrate fertiliser.

I did a lot of the work alone. My army buddy finally showed up, but he wanted to talk. Yeah, to talk – talk it all over once more. 'Not interested,' I said. He could see how angry I was with him so he shut up and helped me push three vats of liquid nitro methane up the truck ramp. Then we had to transfer shock tube and cannon fuse into the truck and some highly explosive Tovex that was shaped like sausage. I was worried this whole truck bomb I was making would blow up before we got to our target.

We parked out beside this lake in a state park. There I mixed nitro methane fluid with each of my fifty-pound bags of fertiliser. Soon I had all these big black barrels in the hold of the truck forming the shape of the letter T – I had to distribute the weight, because the bomb now weighed seven thousand pounds. I added seventeen bags of fertiliser, wetted down with fuel oil. At that point a father and son came near, looking at the truck suspiciously. They'd come for some early-morning fishing.

I didn't want them tipping off the cops. If they'd lingered a bit more I would have shot the dad and dumped him in the lake with a weight around his ankle.

James   And the son?

Harrison (*shifting about uncomfortably*)   I didn't want to kill the kid. I thought I could bind and gag him and hustle him into a motel room and leave him there and by the time they found him I'd be far from there . . . But he and his father left on their own – I think they weren't getting any nibbles. I was so relieved.

James   When did you drive to Oklahoma City?

Harrison   That was the next day. We were up in Kansas. My buddy drove off to his home and I stopped and bought forty dollars' worth of gas and headed down into Oklahoma. I slept in a motel that night and parked my big bomb outside the room. I was still eating these MRE provisions from my Gulf War days.

The next day, D-Day, I entered Oklahoma City at 8.50 a.m. – it was a bright sunny day. It was eerie for me, all these smiling people, especially since I'd turned off the sound – I had earplugs in. I drove up to the Murrah Building, which I'd chosen because it housed both the local FBI and the ATF offices –

James   And a lot of low-level functionaries.

Harrison (*getting angry*)   I don't give a shit about their rank! They worked for the fuckin' Feds. For me it's a civil war and they're enemy soldiers. (*Forcing himself to calm down.*) Let me just stick to the facts. At a stop light a few blocks away from the target I lit the five-minute fuse. It got so smoky in the cab I had to crack the window – my eyes were burning. Then about a block away at another traffic signal I lit the two-minute fuse. I found an empty parking space right in front of the building.

I started to walk away at a fast pace but not running, nothing suspicious, counting out the seconds to myself. I saw a cop car at the corner – it seemed to be empty. I reached the parking lot behind the YMCA where I'd parked my getaway car. Now I was down to zero and the truck hadn't blown yet and I thought, shit, am I going to have to – and then it blew. The ground under my feet registered the blast, I was lifted an inch in the air, some of the falling debris cut a live wire which came whipping across the parking lot toward me. The plate glass in the windows near me was falling in jagged pieces. Even with my earplugs in, the noise was so deafening I couldn't hear anything. I jumped into my getaway car and turned the key – and the damn thing wouldn't start! It stank of gas. I kept nursing it and at last it turned over and I headed out of there. I didn't want to be caught alive in Oklahoma City.

James   What were you feeling?

Harrison   Good . . . cool . . . relieved. I'd watered the tree of liberty. Mission accomplished.

I was heading away from the burning, smoking city, which I could see in my rear-view mirror. All these cop cars and fire engines kept streaming past me toward the city. I hadn't switched the licence plates off my car onto my getaway vehicle. I knew I was tempting fate, I guess. And sure enough I was pulled over by a state cop, about twenty minutes out of Perry, a town close to the Kansas border, and they put me in the local jail for driving without a licence plate. There I was in the clink, watching the TV – and that was the first time I saw the damage I'd done to the Murrah Building. At first I was disappointed that part of it was still standing, but then I thought it was more effective that way, gutted but still half standing. I'd killed 168 people and injured 509 more. I'd killed nineteen kids five and younger all in the day-care centre. I hadn't known about the centre, but it wouldn't have stopped me if I had. But then I thought, 'Great, now they'll present me as a baby-killer, a real psycho.'

Soon everything came undone. In the debris they found the axle of the Ryder truck with its serial number stamped on it. They traced it back to the place I'd rented it. They interviewed the guys in the Ryder shop and put together a sketch of me. The FBI agents showed my picture around the area – the motel lady where I stayed that last night identified me. Now they knew my name, they ran a computer check and they found out I was already behind bars.

James   And the rest is history.

Harrison Did you get all that?

James Yes. Thank you for telling me.

That was a miracle of organisation. You thought out all those details, foresaw all those contingencies.

Harrison Well, a lot of luck was involved. (*Bashful.*) But yeah . . . whatever.

James That's the first time you've told anyone all that –

Harrison Right . . .

James How does it feel to get that off your chest?

Harrison I don't know. Sort of disappointing. In my mind it felt bigger . . . more important.

Pause.

But good. That's good you know it. You'll tell everyone I acted alone.

James Would you do it all again? I suppose that's like asking Medea if she'd kill the babies again.

Harrison What do you mean? Why are you talking about babies?

James No, no, I just mean of *course* you'd do it all over: that's your claim to fame – it's what you did. Without it you'd have nothing – by definition. Nothing.

Harrison (*after a long pause*) I'm so tired. The guard will be back in a minute. The next time you see me, tomorrow, I'll be – it'll be my day of execution. Are you still going to come?

James (*doesn't answer*) The press is already gathering from all around the world. On my way in a French reporter I know tried to interview me.

Harrison What'd you say?

James Nothing. I even denied I was here to see you.

Harrison What will you say?

James   I will say that you had thought the federal government was the guilty party –

Harrison   'I had thought'? Oh, I see. You're already talking about me in the past tense.

James   If they ask if you were sorry?

Harrison   Tell them I was sorry so many people had to die but that I'm not repentant – I wasn't repentant. I acted out of principle, not with respect to individuals. I fought this war the way every soldier has to fight every war. The way they taught me to fight their Gulf War.

James   So this is goodbye?

Harrison   Yep.

James   Was it a mistake for me to come?

Harrison   Was it for you?

James (*slowly*)   No. Not at all.

Harrison   Why are you smiling?

James   I'm just wondering if you have any unasked questions? Here we are – we won't see each other again. Is there anything you want to ask me.

Harrison   No. Nothing. (*Smiles.*)

James   Why are you smiling?

Harrison   We're in a strange situation, aren't we? This may be my last conversation with another human being. If I'm ever going to be honest, this is it.

Pause. Then stamps his foot.

Shit!

James   What?

Harrison   Even so, it's hard to talk!

Squints his eyes shut in an act of resolution.

OK. Here goes. If you could get at me, if there wasn't this plastic wall –

James   Yes?

Harrison   What would you do?

James   What do you mean?

Harrison (*socks his fist in his hand*)   C'mon, man, you started this.

James   All right . . . All right, I'd hypnotise you and then, when you couldn't resist or object, and you wouldn't remember anything when you woke up, I'd hold you in my arms and I'd kiss you.

Harrison (*eyes still squeezed shut*)   And?

James   If I thought you'd never know, I'd unzip that orange jump suit just a bit so I could see your chest. Touch it.

Harrison   And?

James   And nothing.

Harrison   That's it?

He opens his eyes.

James   Are you disappointed?

Harrison   No. Not at all. Kind of relieved.

So, do you have a question?

James   I was going to ask you if you ever had sex with anyone?

Harrison (*laughs indignantly*)   Goddam, back on that old one. (*Very seriously.*) This is not for publication, right?

James   Right.

Harrison   Well then: no. I never got around to that. I never had any really cool pickup lines to get girls. I'd just turn red if I started talking to some babe in the bar. Anyway, I had other shit to do with my life.

James   So here we are. Thanks for telling me all that. I hope
I didn't – what do you young people say? – I hope I didn't
gross you out when I said I wanted to kiss you and maybe
touch your chest.

Harrison   James?

James   Yes?

Harrison   Don't say anything. Don't say one damn thing.
Just come over here. Against the security window.

James *does so.* **Harrison** *slowly unzips his jump suit down to his
waist and then leans against the other side of the plastic screen.*

Harrison   OK. That's it.

The sound of the buzzer and the guard opening the door. He zips up.

Goodbye.

James   Thank you.

Harrison *exits. He doesn't look back but marches out with military
correctness. The lights come down and single out* **James**.

James (*to the audience*)   That was maybe the most extraordinary
moment in my life. I have another definition of intelligence.
One I forgot to mention to Harrison: the ability to act out of
character. A gift for freedom. For generosity of spirit.

People will say I idealised him, that I was blind to his craziness
and the evil in his heart. He never apologised or even admitted
he did anything wrong.

But for me it wasn't that, finally – it was more his loneliness, his
forlornness. That American loneliness. Is there anything more
lonely than a young American man in his car driving through
the West on his own, his heart bursting with indignation? (*Smiling*)
But I won't go on with my personal fetishes. I just want to
admit that a long time ago I lost my objectivity about Harrison.

But you knew that already.

Lights fade.

Methuen Drama Student Editions

Jean Anouilh *Antigone* • John Arden *Serjeant Musgrave's Dance*
Alan Ayckbourn *Confusions* • Aphra Behn *The Rover*
Edward Bond *Lear* • Bertolt Brecht *The Caucasian Chalk Circle*
Life of Galileo • *Mother Courage and her Children*
The Resistible Rise qf Arturo Ui • *The Threepenny Opera*
Anton Chekhov *The Cherry Orchard* • *The Seagull* • *Three Sisters*
Uncle Vanya • Caryl Churchill *Serious Money* • *Top Girls*
Shelagh Delaney *A Taste of Honey* • Euripides *Elektra* • *Medea*
Dario Fo *Accidental Death of an Anarchist* • Michael Frayn *Copenhagen*
John Galsworthy *Strife* • Nikolai Gogol *The Government Inspector*
Robert Holman *Across Oka* • Henrik Ibsen *A Doll's House*
Hedda Gabler • Charlotte Keatley *My Mother Said I Never Should*
Bernard Kops *Dreams of Anne Frank* • Federico García Lorca
Blood Wedding • *The House of Bernarda Alba* (bilingual edition)
Yerma (bilingual edition) • David Mamet *Glengarry Glen Ross*
Oleanna • Patrick Marber *Closer* • Joe Orton *Loot*
Luigi Pirandello *Six Characters in Search of an Author*
Mark Ravenhill *Shopping and F***ing* • Willy Russell *Blood Brothers*
Sophocles *Antigone* • Wole Soyinka *Death and the King's Horseman*
August Strindberg *Miss Julie* • J. M. Synge *The Playboy of the
Western World* • Theatre Workshop *Oh What a Lovely War*
Timberlake Wertenbaker *Our Country's Good* • Arnold Wesker
The Merchant • Oscar Wilde *The Importance of Being Earnest*
Tennessee Williams *A Streetcar Named Desire* • *The Glass Menagerie*

Methuen Drama Modern Plays

include work by

Edward Albee
Jean Anouilh
John Arden
Margaretta D'Arcy
Peter Barnes
Sebastian Barry
Brendan Behan
Dermot Bolger
Edward Bond
Bertolt Brecht
Howard Brenton
Anthony Burgess
Simon Burke
Jim Cartwright
Caryl Churchill
Noël Coward
Lucinda Coxon
Sarah Daniels
Nick Darke
Nick Dear
Shelagh Delaney
David Edgar
David Eldridge
Dario Fo
Michael Frayn
John Godber
Paul Godfrey
David Greig
John Guare
Peter Handke
David Harrower
Jonathan Harvey
Iain Heggie
Declan Hughes
Terry Johnson
Sarah Kane
Charlotte Keatley
Barrie Keeffe
Howard Korder

Robert Lepage
Doug Lucie
Martin McDonagh
John McGrath
Terrence McNally
David Mamet
Patrick Marber
Arthur Miller
Mtwa, Ngema & Simon
Tom Murphy
Phyllis Nagy
Peter Nichols
Sean O'Brien
Joseph O'Connor
Joe Orton
Louise Page
Joe Penhall
Luigi Pirandello
Stephen Poliakoff
Franca Rame
Mark Ravenhill
Philip Ridley
Reginald Rose
Willy Russell
Jean-Paul Sartre
Sam Shepard
Wole Soyinka
Simon Stephens
Shelagh Stephenson
Peter Straughan
C. P. Taylor
Theatre de Complicite
Theatre Workshop
Sue Townsend
Judy Upton
Timberlake Wertenbaker
Roy Williams
Snoo Wilson
Victoria Wood

Methuen Drama Contemporary Dramatists

include

John Arden (two volumes)
Arden & D'Arcy
Peter Barnes (three volumes)
Sebastian Barry
Dermot Bolger
Edward Bond (eight volumes)
Howard Brenton
(two volumes)
Richard Cameron
Jim Cartwright
Caryl Churchill
(two volumes)
Sarah Daniels (two volumes)
Nick Darke
David Edgar (three volumes)
David Eldridge
Ben Elton
Dario Fo (two volumes)
Michael Frayn (three volumes)
John Godber (three volumes)
Paul Godfrey
David Greig
John Guare
Lee Hall (two volumes)
Peter Handke
Jonathan Harvey
(two volumes)
Declan Hughes
Terry Johnson (three volumes)
Sarah Kane
Barrie Keeffe
Bernard-Marie Koltès
(two volumes)
David Lan
Bryony Lavery
Deborah Levy
Doug Lucie

David Mamet (four volumes)
Martin McDonagh
Duncan McLean
Anthony Minghella
(two volumes)
Tom Murphy (five volumes)
Phyllis Nagy
Anthony Neilson
Philip Osment
Gary Owen
Louise Page
Stewart Parker (two volumes)
Joe Penhall
Stephen Poliakoff
(three volumes)
David Rabe
Mark Ravenhill
Christina Reid
Philip Ridley
Willy Russell
Eric-Emmanuel Schmitt
Ntozake Shange
Sam Shepard (two volumes)
Wole Soyinka (two volumes)
Simon Stephens
Shelagh Stephenson
David Storey (three volumes)
Sue Townsend
Judy Upton
Michel Vinaver
(two volumes)
Arnold Wesker (two volumes)
Michael Wilcox
Roy Williams (two volumes)
Snoo Wilson (two volumes)
David Wood (two volumes)
Victoria Wood

For a complete catalogue
of Methuen Drama titles
write to:

Methuen Drama
A & C Black Publishers Limited
38 Soho Square
London W1D 3HB

or you can visit our website at
www.acblack.com